AF753458

The World of Rocks & Minerals

William B. Rice

Earth and Space Science Readers:
The World of Rocks and Minerals

Publishing Credits

Editorial Director
Dona Herweck Rice

Associate Editor
Joshua BishopRoby

Editor-in-Chief
Sharon Coan, M.S.Ed.

Creative Director
Lee Aucoin

Illustration Manager
Timothy J. Bradley

Publisher
Rachelle Cracchiolo, M.S.Ed.

Science Contributor
Sally Ride Science

Science Consultants
Nancy McKeown,
Planetary Geologist
William B. Rice,
Engineering Geologist

Teacher Created Materials
5301 Oceanus Drive
Huntington Beach, CA 92649-1030
http://www.tcmpub.com

ISBN 978-0-7439-0553-4

© 2007 Teacher Created Materials, Inc.

Printed by: 51497
Printed in: China

Table of Contents

Rock Factory: It's Right Beneath Your Feet

Rocks are found everywhere on Earth. We see them in our yards, in parks, and even just lying in the middle of the road. It is a simple thing to walk outside and find a rock. But have you ever thought about what rocks are and where they come from?

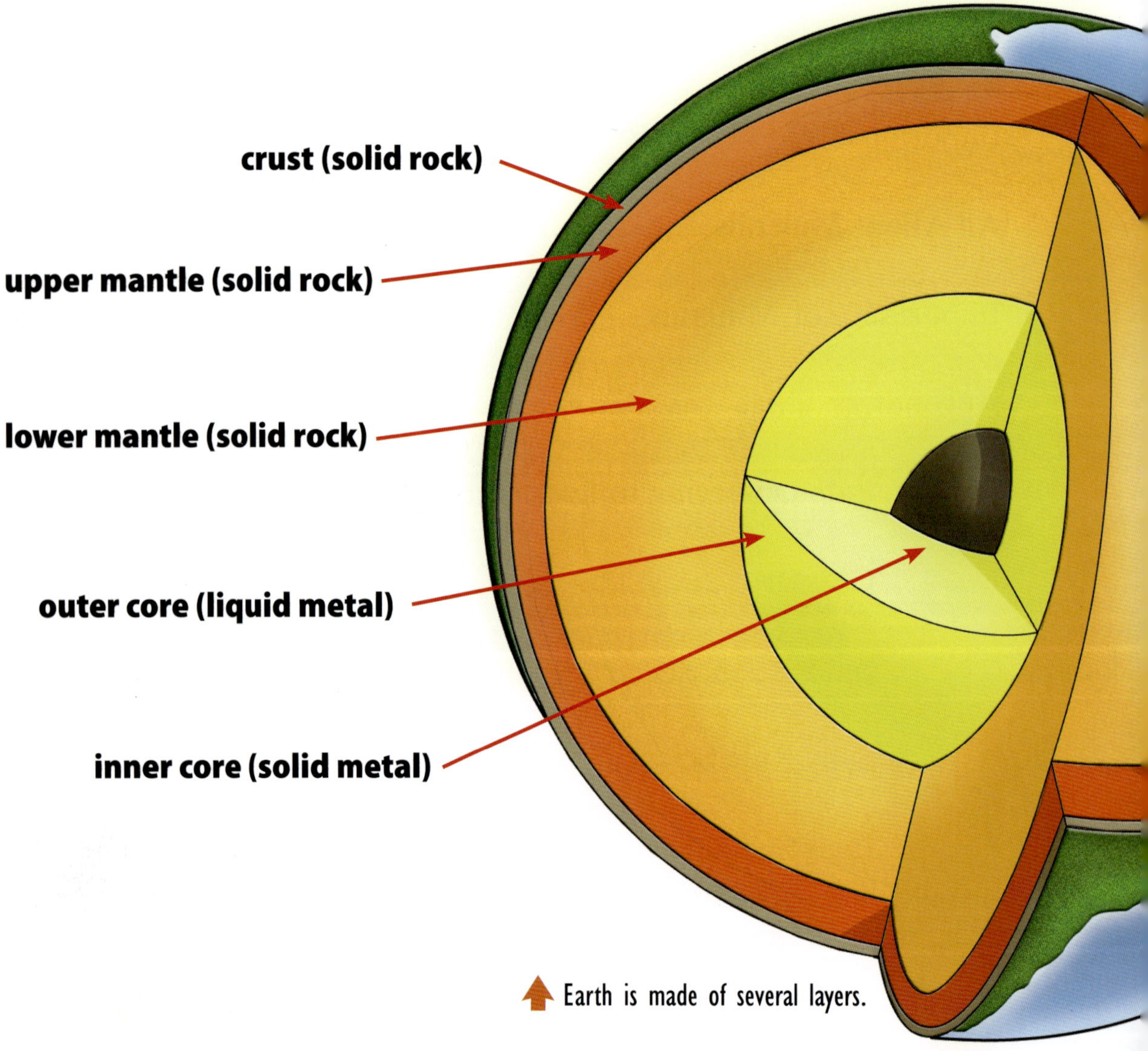

Earth is made of several layers.

There are many different kinds of rocks. They come in an amazing variety of shapes, sizes, colors, and textures. Rocks are not all formed in the same way, though.

Factories use different processes to make things. They use heat, water, and the force from machines to form their products. Our earth is like a giant rock factory. Wherever you are right now, if you could dig down far enough, you would find rocks being made deep inside the earth.

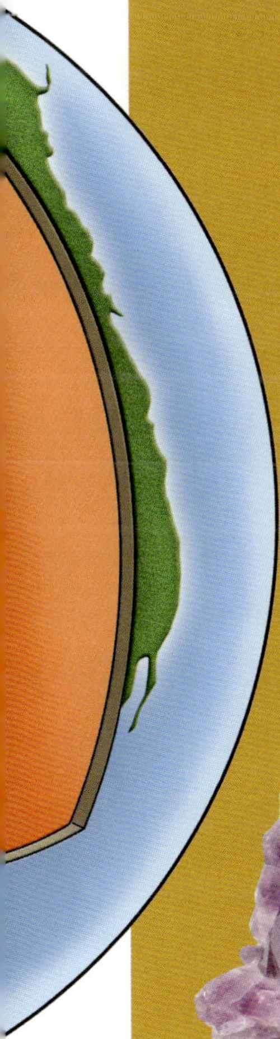

malachite

agate

turquoise

amethyst

opal

Geologists at Mt. St. Helens, Washington, are measuring a crack in the earth's surface.

There are many different kinds of rocks, but they all have some things in common. First of all, rocks are made naturally. Second, they are solid. Rocks are groups of smaller **particles** and **minerals** that are stuck together. Minerals are naturally occurring substances that Earth or organisms on Earth produce. They form **crystals** and are made of specific chemicals.

Rocks can be divided into three rock types: **igneous**, **sedimentary**, and **metamorphic**. These groups reflect the different conditions under which rocks are made.

You will learn what makes each group of rock different, and also the things they all have in common.

quartz crystal

table rock formation in Quebec, Canada

Geologists

Scientists who study the earth are called **geologists**. There are many different types of geologists. They each study different parts of the earth. Here are a few of them.

- Petrologists study rocks and how they are made.
- Mineralogists study minerals.
- Hydrogeologists study water in and on the earth.
- Geomorphologists study how natural processes shape the land over time.

Igneous Rocks

Igneous rocks form from Earth materials that have melted to a liquid called **magma**. Magma usually forms deep beneath the earth's surface where it is very hot.

Some types of magma are thin and runny. They are like water or syrup. Other magmas are thick and gooey. They are like molasses. Magma often gets pushed toward the earth's surface. It squeezes through cracks and holes in solid rocks.

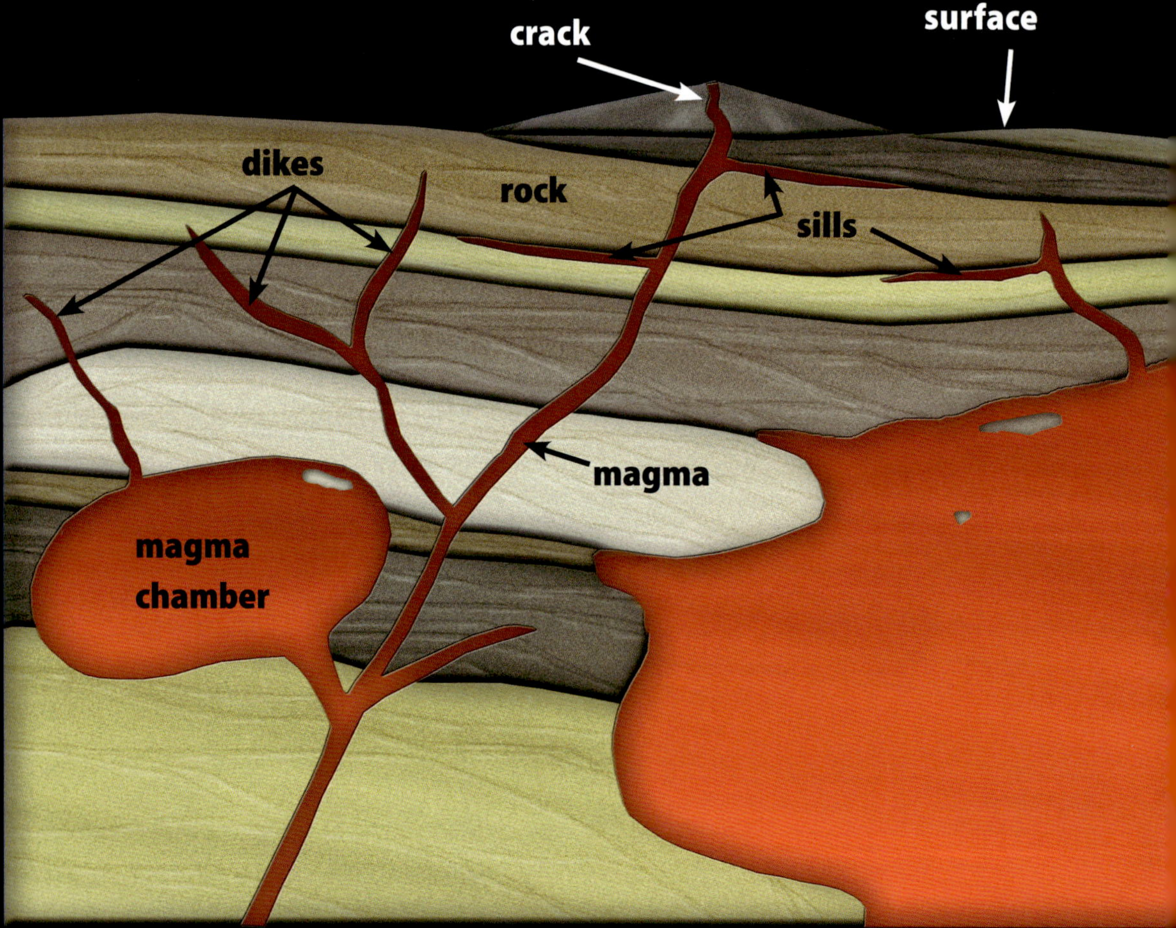

Magma rises from below Earth's surface upward through cracks and fissures. It comes in either oozing or explosive eruptions.

Eruption!

Sometimes when magma rises toward the surface, it gets trapped. Pressure builds up. When the pressure gets too high, a **volcano** can **erupt**. This happened in 1991 at Mt. Pinatubo in the Phillipines. That eruption was the second biggest one of the past century. Lots of gases and dust were blown high into the air. The effects of the eruption killed hundreds of people.

Volcanic eruptions such as this one at Mt. Kilauea in Hawaii can be dangerous but also beautiful.

Extrusive Rocks

When magma reaches Earth's surface, it is called **lava**. After running onto the surface, the lava cools down. It becomes hard. Rocks made in this way are called volcanic or **extrusive** rocks. **Basalt** is one common example of this kind of rock.

Thin magma makes large, gently sloping volcanoes such as those in Hawaii. Thick magma makes smaller but more explosive volcanoes such as Mt. St. Helens in Washington.

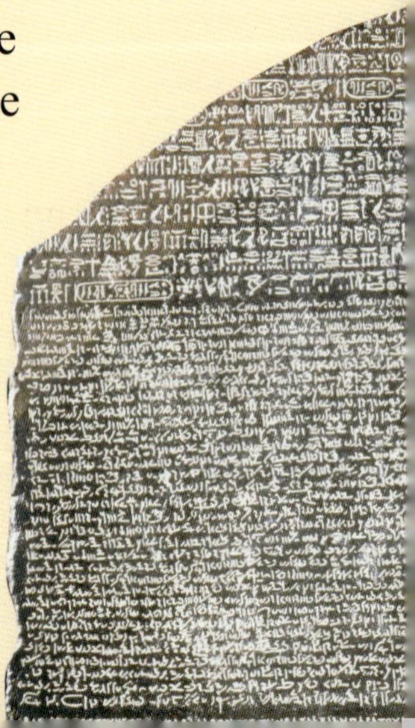

Intrusive Rocks

Sometimes magma cools before it gets to the surface. It cools in cracks and holes in solid rocks. Other times the magma cools in huge underground chambers, which can sometimes be up to 150 kilometers (100 miles) across.

As the magma cools, minerals contained within the magma form crystals. The longer it takes for the magma to cool, the larger the crystals will be. When the magma cools enough, it becomes solid rock made entirely of crystals. These types of rocks are called plutonic or **intrusive** rocks. **Granite** is a common intrusive rock.

If intrusive rocks form underground, how can we see them? Rocks and dirt that cover the intrusive rocks can erode over time, uncovering the intrusive rock.

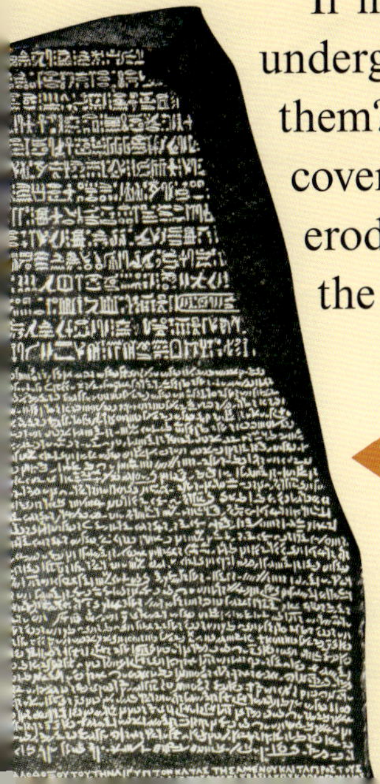

The famed Rosetta stone, created in 196 B.C. is composed of three languages carved into basalt.

Erosion

Erosion is the process of water and wind wearing down rock and carrying away the pieces. Rocks and landforms can change shape from **erosion.**

Granite is a kind of intrusive rock. Its crystals can usually be seen with the naked eye.

Sedimentary Rocks

At the earth's surface, rocks are affected by weather conditions. They are subjected to rain, ice, snow, and wind. They can also be exposed to chemicals, plants, animals, and people. Very hot or cold temperatures can affect rocks, too.

These conditions cause rocks to break into large and small pieces, called **particles**. Particles have different names based on their size. As a group, particles of broken rock that are deposited as **strata** are called **sediment**. Strata are layers of rock and soil in the earth. The chart on the right shows the names given to the different sizes of sediment.

Flowing water contains a lot of energy. Sometimes, swiftly flowing water picks up these sediments. The water carries the

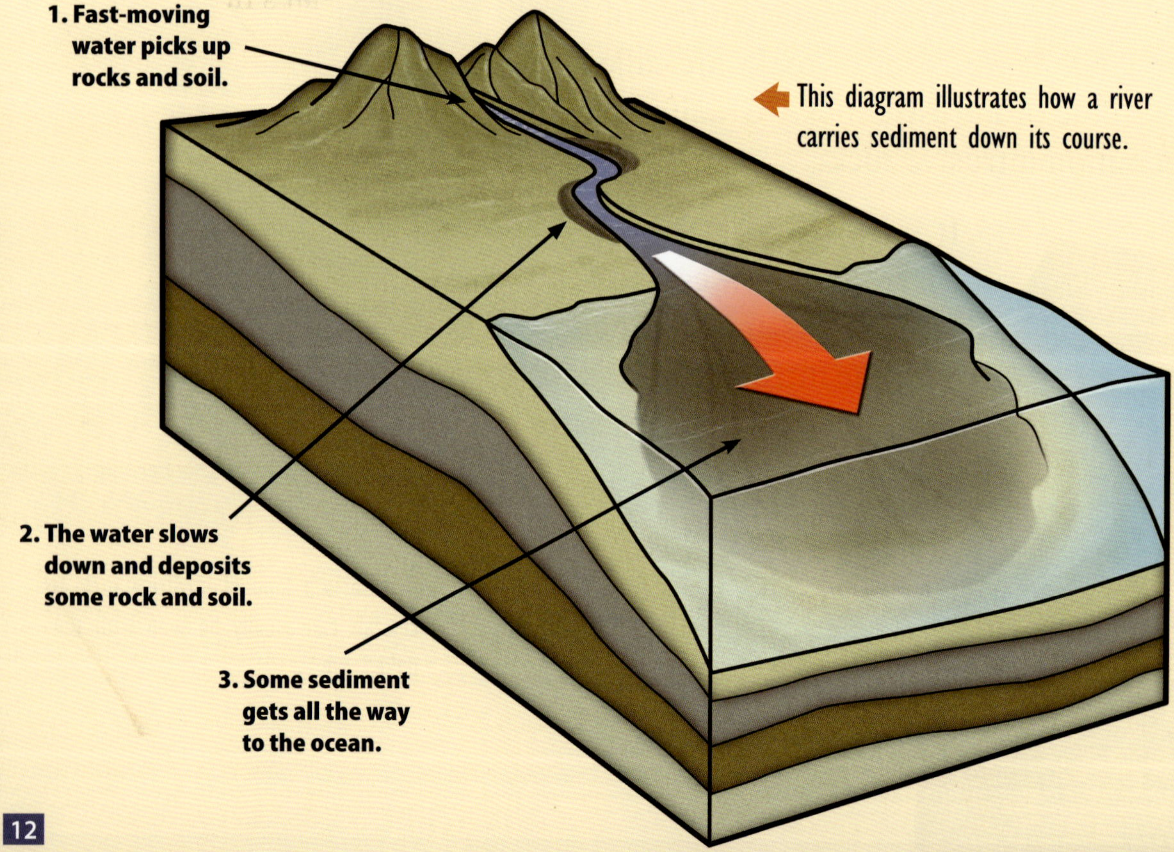

This diagram illustrates how a river carries sediment down its course.

Fun with Fossils

Have you ever found a rock that looks like a bone or that has the print of a plant on it? These rocks are called **fossils**. Fossils can be made when sediments quickly cover animals that have died. Over millions of years, an animal's bones and teeth can be turned into rock. Fossils can tell us a lot about what kinds of creatures once lived on Earth. We know about fascinating animals from long ago by finding their fossils. For example, that's how we learned about dinosaurs and saber-toothed cats.

sediment away. The bigger pieces are heavier, so they do not go very far. But the smaller pieces can be carried a long way. As the water's energy decreases, it drops the sediments back to the ground. This process is called **deposition**. Deposition happens in rivers, streams, and lakes, and at the ocean. There you will see rocks and smaller particles that have been brought there by the force of flowing water.

Sediments

Size	Particle Name
house, car	boulder
football, apple	cobble
peanut, marshmallow	pebble
grains of sugar, grains of salt	sand
flour or dust	silt or clay

exposed layers of sedimentary rock

When rock particles are dropped by water, other sediments can cover the particles. This often happens in oceans and lakes. After a long time, they can be buried under hundreds or even thousands of feet of sediment. That much sediment is very heavy, which puts high amounts of pressure on the lowest layers. There can be so much pressure that the particles get squeezed together and form new rocks. Rocks made in this way are called sedimentary rocks.

The Grand Canyon was carved through many layers of sedimentary rocks.

Skeleton Rocks

There is another kind of sedimentary rock, but it is not made of rock particles. It is made of the hard parts of animals that lived in the ocean. These parts include shells and skeletons. Some of the animals are big, like clams, fish, and lobsters. Some are so tiny that they can only be seen with a microscope. When the animals die, their bodies drop to the bottom of the ocean. There, they can pile up in the same way that rock particles do. Over thousands or millions of years, pressure squeezes them together into new rock called limestone.

Sedimentary Rocks

Made Of	Name
pebbles and cobbles	conglomerate
sand	sandstone
silt and clay	shale

The layers of sedimentary material are easily seen in this small canyon. The canyon was created by wind and water erosion.

Metamorphic Rocks

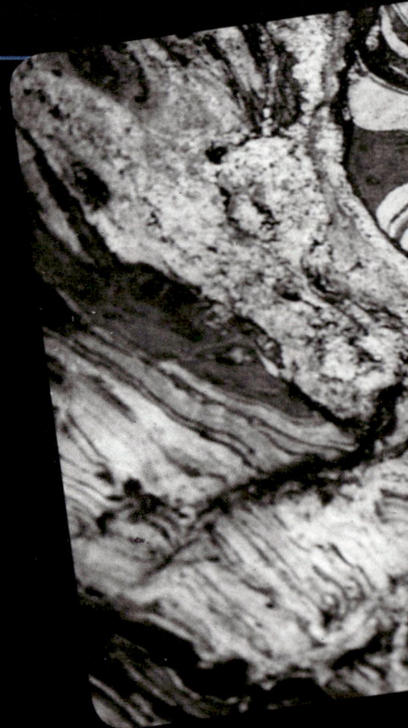

Deep underground, high pressure or heat or both can force rocks such as sandstone or granite to change. They might liquefy and turn into magma, or they might melt just a little bit, cool down, and then become solid again. Because they were not melted completely, they don't become magma. They are now called metamorphic, which means something that has changed. (In this case, a rock.) Some examples of metamorphic rocks are schist, gneiss, and quartzite.

quartzite

banded gneiss injected with granite

specimen of folds in a schist

Write On!

Long ago, children in schools didn't use paper every day. They still needed something to write on, though. Students sometimes carried their own small chalkboards. These chalkboards were actually made of **slate**—a type of metamorphic rock.

Slate begins its life as shale. Heat and pressure change it. The rock becomes metamorphic, turning it into slate. Slate makes good writing material because it is smooth, flat, and dark in color—perfect for chalk to write on. (And chalk is a kind of rock, too!)

Importance and Use of Rocks

Rocks have been important to people throughout history. They have been used to make buildings, walls, and roads. They are also important because of the many different minerals in them. These minerals can be used in many ways. It is important to know what kinds of rocks contain which minerals and where to find those rocks. If you wanted to find diamonds, you would need to know what type of rocks contain diamonds.

Rocks can also hold information that teaches us about the past. That information is in the form of fossils. Fossils tell us what kinds of animals and plants have lived on Earth, and what the earth was like long ago. Rocks themselves contain structures that can tell us similar things. We can also tell from them what Earth might be like in the future.

This diamond has been cut so that it sparkles and can be sold as a jewel.

This diamond is in its natural state.

rock wall

Workers in Vietnam unload coal cars.

Rocks That Burn

Coal is a kind of rock that is made from dead plants that have been buried for many years. People found that coal can burn and produce energy. Coal is used to make electricity and to heat buildings. Since coal is formed under the earth's surface, people and machines must dig for it in mines.

Marble

Marble is a type of metamorphic rock that is formed from limestone. Thin lines and swirls run through the stone, making beautiful patterns. Because of the way it looks, marble is often used for decorations in buildings. The purest marbles are usually white and do not have lines. This kind of marble may be used to create sculptures.

All About Minerals

All rocks are made of minerals, but how are the minerals themselves formed? They are made of chemical **elements**. Elements join together to form minerals. Oxygen and silicon are two examples of elements. Together they form silica, which is commonly called quartz. Each type of mineral is made from a unique combination of elements.

Earth creates minerals in a natural process. Most minerals form when magma cools down or when a rock is changed by pressure and heat. There are even a few minerals that can be formed chemically in water.

Minerals are solid and made of crystals. Different crystals form in different shapes. Some minerals make crystals in the shape of cubes. Others take the shape of pyramids. Some crystals have six or eight sides. Others have fourteen or even eighteen sides! However, each kind of mineral always forms a specific shape with the same type of crystal. Each kind of mineral also has its own level of **hardness**.

white agate with crystals of iron oxide

geode

quartz

Testing for Hardness

Hardness is an important aspect of minerals. A scientist created a way to rate the hardness of a mineral based on a scratch test. It is called the **Mohs Hardness Scale**. Talc is considered the softest mineral, so it is given a hardness level of 1. This is because every other mineral can scratch it. A mineral with a hardness level of 3.5 can be scratched with a penny. Minerals rated under level 5.5 can be scratched with a butter knife. Minerals with a hardness level of over 6.5 can scratch glass. Diamond is the hardest mineral. It has been given a hardness rating of 10. No other mineral can scratch it.

You can scratch gypsum with your fingernail. Quartz can scratch glass. A diamond is the hardest mineral of all.

Quartz is one of the most common minerals on Earth. It is made of the elements silicon and oxygen. It forms when magma underground cools and makes six-sided crystals. Small parts of quartz make up many sedimentary rocks, because it is so common and hard.

Because of its hardness, quartz is a very useful mineral. It is used in jewelry and in concrete. It is used to make glass, too. And since it is so hard, quartz is used in sandpaper.

Galena is also a common mineral, but not as common as quartz. It forms in areas where there is a lot of hot water flowing through cracks in rocks. Hot water can dissolve many minerals. When the water cools, the minerals can form crystals.

Galena usually forms shiny, silver, cube-shaped crystals. Unlike quartz, it is not very hard. Galena often contains lead and silver.

galena

black lava beach sand with green olivine gemstone

quartz

Olivine is also a common mineral. It is nearly as hard as quartz. Olivine is made of the elements magnesium or iron, silicon, and oxygen. It is found mainly in dark, igneous rocks such as basalt. Olivine forms many-sided crystals. Its color is yellow-green or dark green. Some kinds of olivine are used as **gemstones**.

Windows of Rock

Long ago, glass was expensive and hard to get. Sometimes, large sheets of a mineral called **mica** could be found. Mica forms layered crystals like the pages of a book. The layers are thin, flexible, and translucent. Even though mica is not completely clear, the sun can shine through it. Mica was a useful material to use for windows when glass was too expensive for many people to buy. It kept out rainy weather and bugs.

Garnet is a common, hard mineral that can be found mainly in metamorphic rocks. Garnet forms crystals that are something like a cube, but more complex, with many sides. It can be found in a wide spectrum of colors, but most often it is either red or brown. Garnet is commonly used as a gemstone. If you were born in January, then it is your birthstone.

Halite is another common mineral. Most likely, you have some in your own kitchen. Halite is soft. It has cube-shaped crystals. When salty water evaporates, halite is left behind. Another name for halite is salt.

The Dead Sea in Israel is the saltiest sea on Earth. You can see halite deposits on the rocks around the water.

Gemstones

Gemstones are minerals that can be cut and polished for use in jewelry. Here are a few popular gemstones as well as a list of birthstones by month. Which is your favorite?

Diamonds are the most popular gemstone. They are mainly clear, but some are colored pink and yellow.

Corundum is a mineral that comes in different colors. When it is transparent and deep red in color, it is a ruby. When it is transparent and a deep blue, it is a sapphire.

Emeralds are a form of the mineral called beryl. When beryl is transparent and deep green in color, it is an emerald.

Birth Month	Gemstone
January	garnet
February	amethyst
March	aquamarine
April	diamond
May	emerald
June	pearl
July	ruby
August	peridot
September	sapphire
October	opal
November	topaz
December	turquoise

Importance of Minerals

Minerals are important because people use them to make things they need. Some minerals are used to make buildings, windows, and televisions. Others are used to make computers, telephones, and cars. Minerals are used in concrete and steel. They are also used to make jewelry. Minerals are a big part of our everyday lives.

Even the human body needs minerals to survive. Minerals such as iron and calcium keep us strong. Iron strengthens our blood. Calcium is used to make bones. We get many important minerals by eating good food and by taking vitamins.

Coins are made from metals found in different minerals.

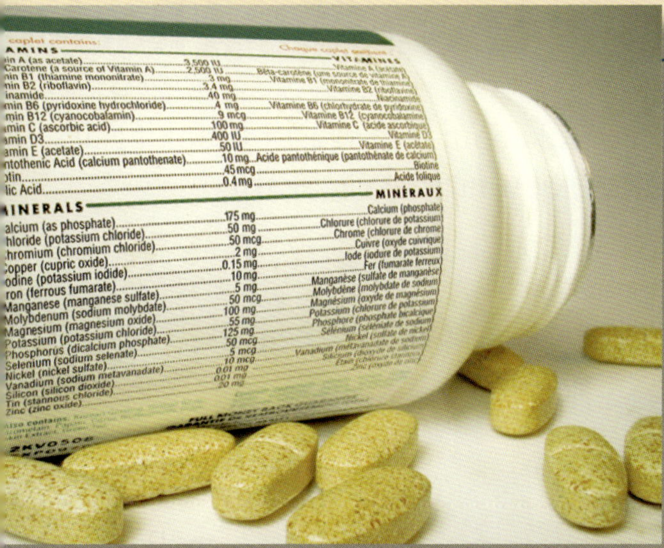

Every healthy body needs daily minerals.

Water Deposits

Minerals can be found in water, too. To see them, just put water in a pan and let it boil away or evaporate. You will find that a white material has been left behind called **water deposits**. The **water deposits** are made of minerals. In fact, we can get many of the minerals our bodies require just by drinking water.

These minerals separate, or precipitate, out of the water in this hot spring.

Some watches are made with quartz. Quartz is a mineral.

Lab: Observing to Learn About Rocks

You can learn a great deal about rocks just by looking at them. Follow these steps to see what you can learn.

Materials

- five different rocks
- water
- magnifying glass
- notebook
- pen or pencil

Procedure

1 You will need to find five different rocks in nature. It is important that they are different. Look around outside in different places. Find them in widely different areas. In your notebook, record where you find each one.

2 Wash each rock in water, one at a time. Look at each rock when it is wet. Observe what it looks like. Pay attention to details. Use the magnifying glass to help you see better. What do you see? Record your observations. Here are some things to notice in particular:

- the color or colors
- presence of crystals

- size and shape of crystals or particles
- shininess of crystals or particles
- amount of one kind of crystal or particle compared to others

3 Look again at each rock when dry. Pay attention to the details again. What do you see? Record your observations. Use the same list as above.

4 Where did you find each rock? What does its location tell you about the rock? Did you find it in a stream bed? Was it on a mountain or valley? Was it in a field, by a lake, or at the ocean? Was there anything important near where you found the rock that might have affected it?

Conclusion

Geologists ask themselves many questions when studying the earth and rocks. In order for you to learn about and identify rocks, you'll want to ask lots of questions like the ones listed above. If you want to study rocks even further, you can also test them for hardness or conduct chemical testing. You will need special tools and a lab for these sorts of tests. With the right tools and the right teacher, you can learn many things about the world of rocks and minerals.

Glossary

basalt—a type of black rock that comes from volcanoes

crystal—a solid formed by the solidification of a chemical and having a highly regular atomic structure

deposition—the geological process whereby material is added

element—a pure chemical substance; the fundamental material of which all matter is made

erosion—condition in which the earth's surface is worn away by the action of water and wind

erupt—to burst or ooze onto the surface

extrusive—igneous rock formed from lava that has flowed out onto the earth's surface, characterized by rapid solidification and grains that are so small as to be barely visible to the naked eye

fossils—any evidence of former prehistoric life

galena—a gray mineral that often contains lead

garnet—a hard, dark-red mineral that is often used in jewelry

gemstone—a crystalline mineral that can be cut and polished for jewelry

geologist—someone who studies rocks and minerals and the structure of the earth

granite—plutonic igneous rock having visibly crystalline texture; generally composed of feldspar, mica, and quartz

halite—naturally occurring crystalline sodium chloride (salt)

hardness—the relative resistance of a mineral to scratching, as measured by the Mohs scale

igneous—rock formed by cooled magma

intrusive—igneous rocks formed by the cooling and solidification of magma beneath the earth's surface

lava—hot liquid rock that comes out of the earth through a volcano or mid-ocean ridge

magma—molten rock in the earth's crust

metamorphic—rocks that are changed by heat and pressure

mica—a natural, glass-like substance that breaks easily into thin layers and is not damaged by heat

mineral—a chemical substance that is formed naturally in the ground

Mohs Hardness Scale—a scale for classifying minerals based on relative hardness, determined by the ability of harder minerals to scratch softer ones

olivine—a mineral consisting of magnesium or iron silicate; a source of magnesium

particles—an extremely small piece of matter

quartz—a very common, hard, glossy mineral consisting of silicon dioxide in crystal form

rocks—the dry, solid part of the earth's surface, or any large piece of this that sticks up out of the ground or the sea

sediment—any matter made of particles that can be transported by fluid flow

sedimentary—made from sediment left by the action of water, ice, or wind

slate—a fine-grained metamorphic rock that splits into thin, smooth-surfaced layers

strata— a horizontal layer of rock, earth, or similar material

volcano—a hill or mountain formed by the extrusion of lava or rock fragments from magma below

water deposits—a white material that is left after water boils away or evaporates; made up of minerals

Index

Sally Ride Science

Sally Ride Science™ is an innovative content company dedicated to fueling young people's interests in science. Our publications and programs provide opportunities for students and teachers to explore the captivating world of science—from astrobiology to zoology. We bring science to life and show young people that science is creative, collaborative, fascinating, and fun.

Image Credits

Cover: Kwan Fah Mun/Shutterstock; p.3 Photos.com; p.4 (top) Photos.com; p.4–5 Tim Bradley; p.5 (top to bottom) Anyka/Shutterstock; Photos.com; Craig Wactor/Shutterstock; (bottom left) Piotr Majka/Shutterstock; (bottom right) Photos.com; p.6 (top) USGS; p.6 (bottom) Robert St-Coeur/Shutterstock; p.6 (background) Liv friis-larsen/Shutterstock; p.7 Photos.com; p.7 (right) Mike Morley/iStockphoto; p.8 (top) ARTSILENSEcom/Shutterstock; p.8 (bottom) Tim Bradley; p.9 David Harlow/US Geological Survey/Time Life Pictures/Getty Images; p.9 (right) USGS; p.10 (top) USGS; p.10–11 Photos.com; p.11 (top) Alison Kriscenski/iStock Photo; p.11 (bottom) Photos.com; p.12 (top) Dwight Smith/Shutterstock; p.12 (bottom) Tim Bradley; p.13 (left) Louie Psihoyos/Getty Images; p.13 (right) Ismael Montero Verdu/Shutterstock; p.14 (top) Dwight Smith/Shutterstock; p.14 (bottom) Photos.com; p.15 (top) Falk Kienas/Shutterstock; p.15 (bottom) Jim Lopes/Shutterstock; p.16 (top) USGS; p.16 (bottom) Nicholas Peter Gavin Davies/Shutterstock; p.16–17 (top) USGS; p.16–17 (bottom) USGS; p.17 (right) Ingvald Kaldhussater/Shutterstock; p.17 (top) Lagui/Shutterstock; p.18 (top) Photos.com; p.18 (right) Scott Rothstein/Shutterstock; p.18 (bottom) Anthony Bannister; Gallo Images/CORBIS; p.18–19 Jenny Matthews/Alamy; p.19 (left) Photos.com; p.19 (top) Kirsty Pargeter/Shutterstock; p.19 (bottom) Photos.com; p. 20 (top) Wilson Valenti/iStockPhoto; p.20 (bottom) Photos.com; p.20–21 Ricardo Miguel Silva Saraiva/Shutterstock; p.21 (left) Photos.com; p.21 (top right) Piotr Przeszlo//Shutterstock; p.21 (center right) Kwan Fah Mun/Shutterstock; p.21 (bottom right) Sebastian Kaulitzki/Shutterstock; p.22 GC Minerals/Alamy; p.23 (top) Samuel Acosta/Shutterstock; p.23 (right) PHOTOTAKE Inc./Alamy; p.23 (bottom) John Henshall/Alamy; p.24 (top) Alexander Maksimov/Shutterstock; p.24 (left) Peter Kovacs/Shutterstock; p.24 (bottom) Photomediacom/Shutterstock; p.25 Scott Rothstein/Dreamstime.com; p.25 (right) Marc Dietrich/iStockphotos; p.26 (top) Photos.com; p.26 (bottom) Photos.com; p.27 (top) Graca Victoria/Shutterstock; p.27 (right) Bernhard Edmaier/Photo Researchers, Inc.; p.27 (bottom) Ewa Walicka/Shutterstock; p.28 (top) Paul Maguire/Shutterstock; p.28–29 Nicoll Rager Fuller; p.32 Getty Images